Dear Student

Dear Student

Alaine Thomson Buchanan

GlossaHouse
Wilmore, KY
www.glossahouse.com

Dear Student by Alaine Thomson Buchanan

Published by GlossaHouse, LLC

GlossaHouse, LLC
110 Callis Circle
Wilmore, KY 40390

Publisher's Cataloging-in-Publication Data

104 pages, vi ; 19.8cm

ISBN: 978-1636630045 (paperback)

Library of Congress Control Number: 2020946504

Book Description: *Dear Student* is a compilation of letters written from a professor to anonymous students that covers a variety of different issues they face, yet written pointedly from a professor's perspective. From the beginning of the semester to the end of the semester, from interacting with professors to dealing with procrastination, from following instructions to taking the feedback from professors in stride—it's all addressed. A short section treats what it's like to be a female minister who teaches in the field of Biblical Studies. Whether you are a professor, an administrator, a parent, a student, a former student, or a future student, this book was written with you in mind.

Printing in the United States of America, First printing, 2020

The fonts used are available from www.linguistsoftware.com/lgku.htm.

Typesetting by Fredrick J. Long
Cover design by T. Michael W. Halcomb
www.glossahouse.com

Contents

Dear Student

Introduction

Dear Reader,

Welcome to "Dear Student"! It's an honor to have you here. Normally, at the beginning of a class, we would do an introduction of some sort, so here are some things you should know about me. I'm a follower of Jesus, an advocate, a minister, an adjunct professor, an active duty military spouse and a mom. Because my family and I move somewhere different every two-three years, I have had the opportunity to serve as an adjunct professor of Bible, Biblical Interpretation and Biblical Theology at the undergraduate, graduate and doctoral levels for schools located all across the United States.

My students have come from various religious backgrounds and countries around the world. I am an avid fan of all things connected to tea, chocolate and the city of Seattle. The Seattle Sounders, Seahawks and Mariners are my favorites, and I am hoping the military keeps us in the area long enough to watch the Kraken. My favorite places to be are at the ocean and in the mountains, and I still dream about changing the world someday.

A few years ago, I started writing general "Dear Student" posts on social media because I realized that I kept addressing similar issues on a consistent basis with my students, and I wondered if other professors talk about these things openly and in public. So, I posted one, and then another, and then another. It wasn't too long before I realized that 1) other professors are dealing with the same things, whether they talk about it or not, 2) current and future students would do just about anything to get into the minds of their professors and to understand what they expect from students, and 3) parents and former students enjoy reminiscing on what life was like "back then."

This book is a compilation of several "Dear Student" notes. They are addressed to an anonymous student and cover a variety of different issues students face, yet it is written from a professor's perspective. From the beginning of the semester to the end of the semester, from interacting with professors to dealing with procrastination, from following instructions to taking the feedback from professors in stride, it's all addressed in here. You will also get an inside look into some of the struggles I face as a female minister who teaches Bible.

Whether you are a professor, an administrator, a parent, a student, a former student, or a future student, this book was written with you in mind. May it set you up for success and bring back good memories at the same time.

All the Best,

Rev. Dr. Alaine Thomson Buchanan

For the Beginning of the Semester

Dear Student,

Embrace this journey for what it is. Don't jump too far ahead or you'll miss something you need in order to be successful. Don't fall too far behind or the stress of trying to catch up may overtake the joy of learning and growing. Do your best in all things. Follow instructions. Ask questions. Take feedback seriously but not personally. Learn. Grow. Be.

You've got this! I believe in you!

Sincerely,

A Professor who needs to hear this today too

Dear Student,

One of the most challenging things about going back to school while working and having a family is learning how to adjust to the "new normal." It's a massive task to try to do all three at the same time (among everything else in life), yet no one balances all three perfectly. There has to be some give and take somewhere, which can be incredibly hard to do, yet it is necessary.

For the season you are in school, you will likely sleep a lot less than normal, you'll find yourself being pulled more directions than you ever thought possible, your schooling may conflict with work and family time, and you may need to set specific boundaries for these different things (when I was doing my Ph.D., I made sure we spent dinner together, which was followed by family time, until our son went to bed, which was about two-three hours a day).

Remember that school is vital. It is part of who God has called you to be and what He has called you to do. It is temporary, and it is critical that you complete what you started.

Sincerely,

A Professor who "gets it," who wants you to succeed and who will not extend deadlines unless it's an emergency

Dear New Graduate Student,

Graduate school is a completely different ballgame than undergrad. It takes about a year (for most of us) to make that adjustment. Give yourself grace ... lots of grace. The learning curve is a big one!

Read your syllabus a few times. Read through the required texts and take notes while you're reading. Do your best with your assignments. Do ask questions, and don't be surprised if your professor sends you back to the syllabus, textbooks and resources in response to your questions. Take the feedback you receive from your professors seriously, not personally. Most importantly, pray, breathe, and get it done! You've got this!

Sincerely,

A Professor who has had this conversation about 20 times (in different ways) so far this week, and it's only the first Thursday of the semester

Dear Student,

If you have never met your professor (and even if you have), it's not a good idea to refer to them in your first correspondence as "Hey, (insert first name)." This inadvertently comes across as rude and disrespectful.

It is much wiser to look your professor up on the school website (or just look at the syllabus) and find out what their educational background is.

It's our job to set you up for success. Learning how to correspond with your professors is a great start!

Incidentally, I don't care what you call me outside of the professor/student relationship. It's just important to learn the lingo of higher education.

Sincerely,

A Professor who wants you to be successful relationally, not just academically

Dear Student,

In preparation for the upcoming semester, here are a few things you should be aware of:

1) All of your professors will have earned at least one degree higher than the one you are studying (with the exception of the doctoral level). This means that at the undergrad level, you'll have professors who have earned at least one doctoral degree and some who have earned a master's degree (or two or three). At the masters and doctoral level, all of your professors will either have already earned their doctorate or are close to finishing it (we use the term ABD in the academic world, which means "all but dissertation" for those who are almost done ... but not quite yet).

2) If you are unsure of what you should call your professor, those who have completed a doctoral degree should be called "Dr. ________." If the professor has not completed (or has not started) a doctoral program, it is best to call your professor "Professor ________."

3) If your professor wishes to be called by their first name with or without a title, he or she will tell you. Do not assume that it's okay to be on a first name basis until they let you know it's okay.

Sincerely,

A Professor who gives this talk at the beginning of every single class, regardless of what level it is.

Dear Student,

Before contacting a professor to ask about why you have not yet received a syllabus or any other correspondence regarding a class, please log in to the format of the said class online to see what is already available. Our job is to set you up for success, but there's not much we can do until you log in.

Sincerely,

A Professor who hopes we can start off on the right foot

Dear Student,

As you prepare for this new semester, please know that your professors are praying for you, and we're looking forward to serving you!

Here are some early reminders that will likely help you to be successful as a student:

1) Read the syllabus and follow it. Most answers to questions about the class can be found there.

2) Walk up to your professor (or the TA or class leader) either before or after the first class, introduce yourself, and say, "Hello!" We care about your success, and putting a name and face together is a great start! If your class is online, set up an appointment to meet with your professor.

3) Use a calendar and write down all of your due dates. There are no excuses for late assignments (outside of emergencies). Doing this will put you a step ahead and may potentially help to reduce procrastination.

4) Stay off of social media during class. It's hard to do, but your ability to interact with others and to get better grades will increase.

5) Ask questions (after looking at the syllabus) and listen to the professor's answer. Listen to the questions other students ask and the answers they receive as well. Sometimes we professors end up repeating the same answer to the same question several times with-

in a five-minute span, which is annoying for everyone (staying off of social media during class helps tremendously with this).

6) Listen to how your professor introduces himself/herself. Look at how they sign their emails. That is how they should be addressed in class and through official correspondence.

7) If there's something you believe your professor should know about you, be sure to tell them. Although Jesus is all-knowing, your professors are not.

8) Know that your professors are human, we have been where you are, and we believe in you. You've got this!

Sincerely,

A Professor who believes in you!!!

Dear Student,

Classes will be starting again soon, and your professors are looking forward to meeting you!

As the semester carries on, some of you will be happy with how your classes are going. Some of you will be disappointed. If you find yourself being disappointed with your professor, their feedback, or your grades, the wisest thing to do is to talk to him or her. When you talk to your professor, here are some things to keep in mind:

1) Ask. Do not demand.

Asking a question is far different than demanding something from your professor. As professors, it is our job to give you the opportunity to be stretched and challenged. We know it is not easy, yet we also see what is ahead of you. If we don't prepare you for what lies ahead, we have failed you, the school, and ourselves.

2) Speak respectfully.

Your professor is there to serve you and is also an authority figure. If you speak respectfully, your professor will listen to you. If you speak disrespectfully, any potential grace that may have been offered to you has the likelihood of being diminished or not offered at all.

3) How you treat your professor is indicative of how you (will) treat those above and below you in your vocation.

Most of us who serve as professors have some (or a lot of) leadership experience. We do more than just "teach."

We serve in our communities, interact with other leaders, use our voices to try to make the world a better place, and on and on from there. We've been around long enough to know that what happens in smaller environments is exacerbated in larger environments, and more than anything, we want you to succeed as a person, a follower of Jesus and as one who exudes integrity.

You can do this!!!

Sincerely,

A Professor who thinks charity, respect, and integrity will take you far

Dear Student,

The best way to pass a class is to listen to and interact with your professor, follow the instructions provided, turn assignments in on time, and adapt the feedback provided on those assignments to future assignments. The best way to fail is to do the opposite of this. Please do the former, not the latter.

Sincerely,

A Professor who believes in you

When It Comes to Following Instructions

Dear Student,

Yes, we are three weeks into this semester. If you would like to be successful in class, making sure you have the required textbooks is a great place to start.

Sincerely,

A Professor who assigns textbooks for a reason

Dear Student,

When specific instructions for an assignment are provided in the syllabus as well as on the assignment online…and an announcement is created to highlight the instructions for the assignment, ignorance cannot be claimed.

Sincerely,

A Professor who knows better

Dear Student,

When one chooses to follow the instructions provided for assignments, they will likely be pleased with the final grade for that assignment. When one does not follow the said instructions, they will likely be amazed and surprised by the final grade for that assignment.

Sincerely,

A Professor who is gearing up for a few "pleased" and a lot of "amazed" and "surprised" students next week

Dear Student,

Research requires doing more than simply quoting Scripture. Asking questions about the passage (and the people within, around and behind the passage), digging into the depths of the passage, reading what others (academics) have written about the passage, and giving credit where credit is due is all part of the process of doing research. No, it may not come easy at first, but if you try and practice, the skills you learn will help it to become easier as time goes on.

Sincerely,

A Professor who really wants you to succeed

Dear Student,

Please be careful when using biblical Hebrew, Greek or Aramaic words or transliterations in your paper. Yes, I know all three languages. Yes, I will notice when the wrong word is used. Yes, I will tell you what the correct word is.

Sincerely,

A Professor who teaches "Don't use biblical languages in papers unless you are sure you know the language"

Dear Student,

When research is required for an assignment, it's a good idea to actually include research in your writing. When you only provide your perspective and present it as fact, it is obvious to us that you have not taken the time to discover "more" than your own opinion, which is not good. Do the research, learn, and grow.

Sincerely,

A Professor who requires research for a reason

Dear Student,

When participating in discussion boards, please read and follow the instructions given to you by your professor before posting. If you choose to write an "accidental" initial post so you can see what other students have written in their initial posts and then decide to follow their lead (without reading the professor's instructions first), you may discover that you missed something important in your initial post, and you may not realize that the student(s) you are trying to emulate might not have fully read and followed the instructions either.

Sincerely,

A Professor who sees what's happening and who knows you can do better

Dear Student,

While I can appreciate your straightforward approach in telling me that I was completely unfair in my grading of your assignment, the reality that the instructions were not followed this time suggests that you'll do much better the next time, if you choose to follow the instructions.

Sincerely,

A Professor who thinks a little bit of humility goes a long way

Dear Student,

No one knows exactly what they're doing the first time they try something new. That's why it's important to do your best on your assignments and then learn from the feedback you receive from your professors. All of us have been there before. We believe in you and want you to succeed. Ultimately, the choice to succeed begins with your willingness to try.

Sincerely,

A Professor who knows that success is the result of trying and trying again (multiple times over)

Things to Remember

Dear Student,

In your time as a student, you'll have the opportunity to interact with people from various backgrounds and from various generations. Take every opportunity to learn from someone who is different than you. Expand your horizons. Broaden your capacity to understand and love others. Choose to interact. You may be surprised at the friendships you are able to build when you step out of your comfort zone!

Sincerely,

A Professor who is grateful—so very grateful—
for diversity

Dear Student,

We oftentimes don't know the stories of the people around us, unless they choose to tell us. Let's remember that our words (both spoken and written) have the potential to bring life and hope to someone who desperately needs it, which can then be the impetus for life change. May God help us to see beyond the surface and to call out what is good and true in each other.

Sincerely,

A Professor who needs to be reminded of this
on a daily basis

Dear Student,

Context matters ... a lot. Without taking context into consideration, all sorts of things can be mistaken or misunderstood, and we can easily make assumptions that aren't accurate or true.

With everything going on in our world today, I think it would be wise for us to ask questions, listen, learn and remember that context really does matter ... a lot.

Sincerely,

A Professor who appreciates the value of "context"

Dear Student,

Seeking to understand literature within its context is critical if one wants to apply its meaning to life and ethics today. Failure to do so can result in manipulation of the text that is misappropriated under the guise of one's personal ideology, which is not good.

Sincerely,

A Professor who believes responsibility
and integrity matter

Dear Student,

Lots of people get colds, the flu, migraines, etc., around this time of the year. It's up to you to communicate with your professor that you are sick before assignments are due and to also provide him or her with a doctor's note so that they can leverage more grace for you. If communication happens after an assignment is due and/or a doctor's note is not provided, there isn't as much we can do to help. We want you to be successful, yet your communication is key.

Sincerely,

A Professor who had a migraine last week, has a cold this week, and is still working anyway

Dear Student,

Save your work. Email it to yourself. Save it on Dropbox or on a thumb drive. It doesn't matter to me how you do it. Just save it in multiple places. This will save you from all kinds of trouble, especially when an assignment is due.

Sincerely,

A Professor who repeats the same thing over and over again, only to have students finally listen after it's too late

Dear Student,

Vacations. They are wonderful experiences to look forward to! When you sign up for class and know that you will be going on vacation in the midst of class, get your work done ahead of time. Do not expect the professor to give extensions when it's not an emergency situation.

Sincerely,

A Professor who will also be going on vacation to visit family next month (I only get to see them about once a year) and who will still be teaching, grading and interacting while there

Dear Student,

Sometimes, there is a fine line between confidence and arrogance. When in doubt, confidence coupled with humility is a great option.

Sincerely,

A Professor who greatly appreciates the confidence + humility combination

Dear Student Who is Training for Ministry,

Jesus ate and interacted with those whom the religious elite rejected. He welcomed them to his table. Communion is an invitation, an opportunity from Jesus to enter into a deeper relationship with him. It is sacred space. It is holy ground.

Please do share the gospel message. Do explain what communion is and what it means. Do allow opportunity for wrongs to be made right. Do take a step back and watch God do the things that only God can do.

Please, please, please do not make personal judgment calls about who is and is not "worthy" to participate. Offering the option of not participating or to let the elements pass by is wisdom. Refusing to allow participation is unChristlike.

Sincerely,

A Professor and minister who wants to be more like Jesus and less like the religious elite

Dear Student,

Power, prestige, and influence tend to bring out the best and worst in people. Humility, accountability, and integrity are vital for people to retain their "humanity" when serving in areas of influence.

On a large scale, we're currently seeing the ramifications of what happens when the dark, hidden side of a leader or influencer is exposed to the world at large. It is painful, horrific, and ugly.

At the same time, we can choose to be different. We can choose to do the right thing, even though it's hard. We can choose to invite people into our lives to keep us accountable. We can choose to say, "I was wrong" and to ask for forgiveness. We can choose to acknowledge and address the sins that pull us away from God and from each other. We can choose strong humility when (unhealthy) pride would be the easier option.

When we begin to grasp our humanity and the humanity of the people around us, we realize our desperate need for a Savior. When we choose integrity, humility and accountability, the character of Christ shines through us and extends to those around us. Then, we can point people to Jesus, who deserves all praise, honor, and glory.

Sincerely,

A Professor who wants to become more like Jesus

Dear Student,

In the midst of all the writing of papers, completing projects, and turning in all kinds of assignments, please don't forget that at the end of the day, this education you are participating in is all about people ... understanding them, reaching them, helping them, and "being" with them. It's also about understanding yourself ... who you are, the way you are wired, your strengths and weaknesses, and gaining greater insight into who God created you to be.

If you keep this in mind, you'll be able to transfer whatever it is you are studying into the relationships you have with the people around you, which gives you a greater opportunity to extend Jesus to whoever surrounds you, regardless of who they are, where they are from or what their life situation entails. God is with you!

Sincerely,

A Professor who sees the bigger picture
(most of the time)

Technicalities

Dear Student,

Please proofread your paper/project and do a spelling and grammar check before turning your work in. It will save your grade ... and my sanity.

Sincerely,

A Professor who despises and abhors working with details but does it anyway because student success matters (both now and in the future)

Dear Student,

When writing a paper and interacting with a female scholar, please be sure to acknowledge her as "she," not as "he."

Sincerely,

A Professor who believes women can be phenomenal scholars

Dear Student,

When writing papers (research papers, book reviews, etc.), please write in paragraphs with complete sentences. It will be immensely helpful to your cause ... and to my ability to understand your perspective.

Sincerely,

A Professor who is trying to follow your train of thought

Dear Student,

Although I appreciate the compliment, notes from class do not count as academic research for papers.

Sincerely,

A Professor who is grateful you paid attention in class and who really wants you to do good, solid research for your papers

Dear Student,

12:00 p.m. is not midnight. It is noon. 12:00 a.m. is midnight.

Sincerely,

A Professor who normally has assignments due by 11:59 PM but decided to try something new … and who will now be going back to making assignments due by 11:59 PM.

Dear Student,

Approximately half of my day (so far) has been spent dealing with plagiarism. When a student plagiarizes (even if it's on accident), there are consequences that both you and your professor have to pay. The best course of action is to always, always, always put quotation marks around any quotations you use and be sure to cite the source(s) you are using.

Sincerely,

A Professor who takes plagiarism seriously

Dear Student,

My husband and I are trying to teach our son that the choices we make oftentimes affect other people.

On the way to take him to school today, he asked me why I've had to stay up "into the middle of the night" so many times since school started. We talked about how dishonesty and disobedience are treated at his school, and then I told him that dishonesty and disobedience have much larger consequences when people go on to university and graduate school. The choices that others have made mean that I have to spend a bunch of extra time addressing those situations.

He paused for a moment and then asked if his teacher has to take extra time out of her schedule and out of time with her family when he disobeys or is disrespectful. I said, "Yes, she does."

... and then, I think he understood.

He said, "Mom, I don't want to disobey or be disrespectful, and I don't want my teacher to be sad anymore. I don't want your students to make bad decisions either, and I want them to apologize to you and tell you that they won't ever make the same choices again."

I think the lesson has been learned ... I hope.

Sincerely,

A Professor who is suffering the consequences of plagiarism alongside her students

Dear Student,

As your professor, I will tell you when your writing is not up to par. Writing is about thinking, processing, engaging, and developing ... all at the same time. Yes, it may be hard to hear, and it might be painful. Nevertheless, I will tell you the truth because I believe in you, and I see your potential.

To me, grading is much more than "just giving a grade." It's about helping you move deeper and forward into who God has called you to be and what He has called you to do. YES, I will be the first to cheer loudly for you when you "step forward" into greater success in our class.

Sincerely,

A Professor who looks forward to celebrating your hard work soon

For When Feedback … and Grace Are Offered

Dear Student,

When a professor provides feedback on an assignment, they are not trying to "destroy" you. Rather, they are trying to help you improve in your writing and communication skills, and they are trying to help you reach the "standard" that is set for your class and your educational level.

On another (but similar) note, it's important to be able to separate "who" you are from what you turn in for assignments. If you believe your assignments are directly connected to your value as a person, then you will likely think your value lies solely in what others think about what you "do" rather than on who you "are." This is a dangerous road to travel.

It is much wiser to do your best on your assignments, turn them in on time, and be able to say, "I did my best, and I am valued because of who I am. My grade is important, yet my value does not solely rely on this assignment or this grade."

Sincerely,

A Professor who values you as a person and sees lots of potential for growth

Dear Student,

Reading the instructions is half the battle. Following the instructions is the other half. Ask questions after doing the first half and before turning in the second half. Don't wait to ask questions until the day before (or the day) an assignment is due. If you do these things, you will be successful.

Sincerely,

A Professor who writes instructions for a reason

Dear Student,

Yes, it's true that if you decide not to be involved in class until part-way through the class, you will be lost, especially in classes where assignments build upon each other until they become a final product.

When opportunity after opportunity to succeed has been offered to you, when your professor has reached out to you to try to help you succeed (and there has been no response on your end), and when you choose not to take advantage of the grace that was offered to you, it is not your professor's fault if you fail the class.

Yes, we professors care about you. Yes, we want to see you succeed ... very much so. You are the reason why we do what we do. At the same time, you need to take responsibility for the choices you've made along the way.

I still believe in you!

Sincerely,

A Professor who still wants you to succeed

Dear Student,

When you are in a class where all the assignments build upon each other to create a final product/paper, it is wise to pay attention to the feedback the professor gives to you on each piece of the puzzle. He/She is spending a lot time trying to help you discover how to learn, grow and succeed.

If you choose to ignore that help, the grade for the final product/paper is going to be significantly lower than you think it should be. Do not whine. Do not complain. Learn from this mistake and be sure to accept the help that's offered to you the next time around.

Sincerely,

A Professor who realizes that teaching is a lot like being a parent

Dear Student,

When instructions are laid out, announcements addressing the step-by-step instructions have been made and a grading rubric has been provided to you (and you have not asked questions), there really is no excuse for not following instructions.

Sincerely,

A Professor who is practicing “tough love” at the moment

Dear Student,

When a professor provides feedback on an assignment and tells you what can or needs to be improved the next time around, it's constructive criticism. Your professor doesn't hate or dislike you. Rather, your professor believes in you enough to tell you that there's more to you than what you can see at the moment...and to push you to become a better researcher and writer.

Sincerely,

A Professor who thinks highly enough of you to challenge you to stretch beyond your current capabilities

Dear Student,

When a professor tells you that they will provide feedback once per assignment (when they grade the assignment), that means they will not regrade the said assignment if you try to resubmit it, and they will not provide feedback on your assignment before it is officially turned in.

Do your best, and you'll get there!

Sincerely,

A Professor who knows that if you do "favors" for one, you have to do "favors" for all

Dear Student,

It is wise to pay attention to the feedback professors give to you on your assignments. It's our responsibility as professors to help you become better at your craft ... and believe it or not, we see more in you than you see in yourself right now.

When you take our constructive criticisms in stride and turn in even better work the second time around, we are so proud of you! When our feedback is ignored, it only hurts you in the long run, and it hurts you even more the second and third time around.

When you allow yourself to be stretched and challenged, you will be amazed at what you can accomplish.

Sincerely,

A Professor who cares about you

Dear Student,

You listened and paid attention to the constructive criticism that was provided, you made adjustments, and your final paper is outstanding! I am so proud of you!

Sincerely,

A Professor who is shouting "Yes! Yes! YES!!!" and is giving you a "virtual" standing ovation

Dear Student,

Neglecting to read through the instructions for an assignment and then rushing through the assignment "just to turn something in" is not a good mix. If you expect grace to be extended to you on top of that, well, it just isn't going to happen (unless it's an emergency).

The better route is to plan ahead (aka don't wait until the last minute), read through the entirety of the instructions, ask your professor questions at least two or three or more days before an assignment is due (that's what we're here for), and follow the instructions for the assignment. Doing a quick spelling and grammar check is also necessary (professors do this with their writing too). Take our feedback seriously, and you'll be all set.

Sincerely,

A Professor who know success comes by following instructions

Dear Student,

When a professor offers you a bit of grace regarding turning in late work (aka, You can turn your assignment in late with a reduced grade as opposed to receiving a zero), the best thing to do is to take the grace that is offered and say, "Thank you!" It is not a good idea to complain that the grace extended to you is not enough and to "expect" the professor to give you more.

Take responsibility for your late work. Own it. Turn your assignments in. Being "called by God" does not excuse you from doing the work that is required of you, nor does it excuse you from doing your best. Just as grace can be extended to you, it can also be taken away.

Sincerely,

A Professor who is not a fan of entitlement

Dear Student,

When a professor tells you that you did an assignment incorrectly and offers you the opportunity to do it again (because the assignment is critical for your success in the class) and when the professor provides you an example of what the submitted assignment should look like, here are some things you SHOULD do:

1) Take advantage of the opportunity to try again and to turn the assignment in within the time frame the professor offers to you.

2) Pay attention to the feedback the professor gave to you on the first assignment.

3) Look at the example that was provided for you and make the adjustments.

4) Say, "Thank you for giving me another chance."

DO NOT:

1) Ignore messages from your professor. You just might miss out on something important ... really important.

2) Neglect to pay attention to the feedback your professor gives to you. It's your professor's job to help you learn, grow and succeed. If you choose to ignore their insight and help, you are setting yourself up for failure.

3) Disregard the example that has been provided for you. If a professor shows you what your assignment

should look like (including the various components of the assignment), it is unwise to turn in something vastly different.

4) Whine and complain because you missed or chose not to take the opportunity to "try again."

Sincerely,

A Professor who cares about you and your success both inside and outside of this class

Dear Student,

When a professor is strongly encouraged by the school to give extra grace to you so that you can finish a course AND the professor goes out of his or her way to tell you what needs to be turned in and when (so that you have a solid chance of succeeding), it would be wise to heed that professor's advice.

Do not wait until the day before the extension of grace ends to start asking questions and turning things in. Do not expect that your professor's life revolves around you and your situation (Yes, we do care about you and your situation. We have several other students we care about as well ... not to mention our own families), and do not beg that professor to "make a way" for you to pass the class.

It is vital that you, as a student, take responsibility for what happens on your end. I am here to help you succeed. Sometimes, that means making and upholding solid deadlines.

Sincerely,

A Professor who cares about your long-term success

Dear Student,

If a professor offers you a second chance on an assignment, take it. If you take advantage of this opportunity, make sure you turn in the "right" version of that assignment. Your professor will grade whatever has been turned in and will provide you with feedback.

If you contact the professor after they have graded the second version of your assignment and say, "Oops! I made a mistake and turned in the wrong version of this assignment. Can you please provide feedback on this version?" they will likely give you a (hopefully) nice, but firm, "No."

Sincerely,

A Professor who rarely offers second chances and sometimes regrets doing so

Dear Student,

Grace is costly. While it gives you more time to finish assignments, it often costs professors a significant amount of time and energy that you might not be aware of. Giving grace means we often must find time and space to stop what we're working on (or to sacrifice extra time away from the people we love) to provide you with feedback.

Yes, we professors believe in you, and we do what we do because we want you to succeed. We just appreciate it when grace is asked because of an emergency, not because of lack of timeliness.

Sincerely,

A Professor who believes that deadlines are deadlines (except for emergency situations)

Procrastination …
and the Joy of Emails

Dear Student,

Reading and following instructions are vital for your success. Asking questions about assignments before they are due is a good idea too.

Sincerely,

A Professor who is not a fan of laziness …
or procrastination

Dear Student,

When professors send several emails to offer help, guidance and assistance throughout the duration of the class, take them up on it right away. DO NOT wait until three hours before an extended time of grace ends to say that you don't understand and that you need help. Waiting until the last moment does not help your cause.

Sincerely,

A Professor who believes time management is a key to success

Dear Student,

If you want to succeed, you must follow the instructions for assignments. In order to follow the instructions, you must read the instructions and listen to what your professor says in class. If you have questions about the assignment, ask ahead of time (before the day the assignment is due). Do not arbitrarily turn something in and expect to be pleased with your grade. You are better than this, and you can do better than this too.

Sincerely,

A Professor who believes you are better than this

Dear Student,

Procrastination tends to promote rushing through assignments, neglecting to follow instructions, and unbelievable amounts of stress. On top of that, crazy things tend to happen a day or two before an assignment is due. Sometimes, unexplainable and unexpected things happen the day, hour, or even moments before an assignment is due.

The best way to alleviate all these things is to plan ahead and finish your work at least a day or two or three before the due date. Pay attention to the instructions for the assignment … and follow them. Like I wrote before (and I can't emphasize this enough), save your work regularly, email it to yourself, put it in a Dropbox. Just be sure to save it in multiple places. Do these things, and you'll be so much happier about life ... and about your grades too.

Sincerely,

A Professor who can see procrastination
from a mile away

Dear Student,

Professors have 24 to 48 hours to respond to emails, text messages and phone calls. If you wait to ask a question (or two or ten) until a day before (or the actual day) an assignment is due, you may not get a response in time. That's part of the reason why we encourage you to get started early on your assignments.

Sincerely,

A Professor who is a fan of not waiting ...
until the last minute

Dear Student,

I am so grateful to have you in my class. Please do know that I have received the multiple emails you have sent me over the past 10 hours. Please also understand that it's important to wait 24 to 48 hours for me to respond to your first email before sending me multiple follow-up emails.

Yes, I do care very much about you and your success. I also care about every other student I have the privilege of interacting with.

In the future, please send one email, text message, or phone call, and then trust that I will do my job and get back to you.

Sincerely,

A Professor who is trying to give grace …
and have patience

Dear Student,

When emailing your professor, using phrases like "In all my years of education, I've never ..." don't grab our attention the way you think they might. Most of the time, we've been in school much, much longer.

Sincerely,

A Professor who has been teaching a bit longer than you've been a post-high school student

Dear Student,

Yes, all of us want to know how we did on the assignments we turn in ... and we want to know those grades as soon as possible. At the same time, please do not ask if your major paper has been graded within 24 hours after the assignment is due.

Consider this: For major papers, take the number of pages/word count for your paper and multiply it by the number of students in your class. That is how many pages your professor has to grade and provide feedback on. This is just for your class. Your professor likely has other classes they're teaching and is working on grading those assignments as well.

This is why most schools say that professors should have up to two weeks to turn in grades for major assignments. If you haven't heard from your professor in a week or so, DO ask your professor how they're doing and ask if they've had the chance to look through your paper yet. If they have not, there is likely a really good reason for it. If it's been two weeks or more, then it's okay to send another (polite) email.

As professors, it's our job to provide you with good, solid feedback to help you as you move on in your program. Doing this takes time.

Sincerely,

A Professor who is grading over 250 pages of student writing this weekend

Dear Student,

When asking your professor why your paper (that was due 24 hours ago) has not yet been graded, please keep the following in mind: 1) Usually professors have up to a week to grade smaller assignments and up to two weeks to grade major assignments. 2) Professors do much more than a simple read-through of student papers. We process, assess, grade, and provide insight and feedback on student papers, and we do that for every student, which takes time and energy.

For example, if a professor hypothetically has 15 students in a class, and all students turn in a 10-page paper, that's 150 pages of student writing that the professor needs to provide feedback on within a one-two week period ... and that's just for one class.

Yes, we believe in you. Yes, we are FOR you. Yes, you deserve the time it takes to provide solid feedback.

Sincerely,

A Professor who is thankful for the professors who took a significant amount of time to provide feedback on her writing

Because I Believe in You

Dear Student,

When we first met, you introduced yourself and then immediately stated that you would love to have my job someday. I smiled and said, "That's great! As soon as you fulfill all the necessary requirements and are hired on to teach, I'll step aside for you because ultimately, I believe God is the one who opens up opportunities to teach, speak, preach and lead. When it's time for me to move on, that's what I'll do."

The reality is that sometimes, a person's titles and opportunities seem attractive to someone who does not yet have them and wants them. At the same time, the untold story and the cost behind those things is more than anyone but Jesus will ever know.

My dear student, I've been where you are. I had (and still have some of) the confidence you have, and I can definitely see your potential. If you do choose to pursue this route, get ready. It may cost you everything (or just about everything), yet it has the potential to form the character of Christ within you in ways you have not yet imagined.

For now, it would be wise to listen to your professors, read and follow assignment instructions, complete assignments on time and pay attention to the feedback professors offer to you. By doing these tasks, you will set yourself up to be a successful student, which is necessary if you want to become a professor one day.

Sincerely,

A Professor who believes great students can become great professors

Dear Student,

You complained that I am too hard on you and that I should take your responsibility as a bi-vocational minister into consideration when grading your assignments. You also claimed that I couldn't possibly understand what it's like to hold down a secular job, be a minister, be in school and have a family at the same time.

The truth is that I honestly, truly don't know what it's like to be you, yet it is clear that you are unhappy with your current grades.

There's a lot I could say here about work, ministry, school, family, friends and balance, but what you really need to know is that I see a lot of potential in you. It's my responsibility to pull that out of you and push you to try. If you're not reaching "the standard," it's my job to help you reach it and surpass it. I believe in you and will not apologize for believing in you enough to challenge you to be greater than you think you are right now.

Someday, you'll see the value and the investment of your education. You'll see that your education was much more than a grade. Education is (at least, it should be) an opportunity to learn, grow, and become more conformed to the heart, mind and image of Christ. It's not easy, but it's worth it. You can do it!

Sincerely,

A Professor who sees the bigger picture and knows that God has HUGE plans for you

Dear Student,

We had the most interesting conversation in class today. You told me that I'm very intimidating, which was followed up with, "I just didn't know that females could be strong, straightforward and be a doctor and a minister at the same time." This comment was followed up with, "Maybe God can do amazing things with me too."

I would call this conversation a win.

Sincerely,

A Professor who believes you should dream big …
and go do it

Dear Student,

Your comment in class today made me smile from ear to ear. You said, “So you’re really Rev. Dr. Buchanan? I’ve never heard of a female being a Rev. Dr. before. That is so cool!”

What this really means is that you, too, need to pursue your dreams and help other people achieve theirs.

Sincerely,

A Professor who hopes your life inspires others too

Dear Student,

We had an interesting conversation the other day. You said that my titles and degrees are intimidating and that you are scared of me. I'd like to apologize to you. No, you didn't do anything wrong. I didn't do anything wrong either, yet this apology is still needed.

You see, in some circles, we have deemed that women are sub-par to men, that women are and should be limited in who God has called them to be and what God has called them to do. We are trained to be shocked, surprised, scared and intimidated by someone who does not "fit" within this paradigm. You see, if I was a man with the same titles and degrees, you wouldn't think twice about who I am and what I do ... because that is what is "normal" within some church cultures.

No, I do not blame you for initially reacting to me this way. At the same time, I am sorry that pastors, ministers and other leaders have taught you that you, as a woman, are "less than," that you are "subordinate to" and that you do not matter as much as a man does.

The reality is that you don't have to fit into someone else's paradigm. Break the mold. Climb the mountain. Shatter the ceiling. Listen to Jesus. Follow His lead and move forward. Don't be surprised if God calls you to do something out of the ordinary too.

Sincerely,
Rev. Alaine Thomson Buchanan, Ph.D.
(follower of Jesus, active duty Army chaplain's wife, mom, minister, professor, preacher, public speaker and Bible study writer/teacher)

Dear Student,

You recently asked me if I ever face opposition because I teach Biblical studies at the graduate and undergraduate levels and am a public speaker/preacher, so I hope that in sharing my thoughts with you, it will give others encouragement to keep moving on and keep pushing forward, especially in the unseen and "unknown to everyone else" moments:

Yes, I face opposition on a weekly and sometimes a daily basis, and it's been that way ever since God called me into ministry over 30 years ago. Over the years, I've learned something, though. God is the one who calls, God is the one who opens doors, and God is the one who changes people's lives.

Those who oppose God's calling on my life may be able to slow things down a bit. They may tell me I can't because I'm a woman or because I don't hold a certain status in society, but they can't stop God's work in, for and through me. In other words, their comments and actions have no bearing on God's calling; therefore, I do my best to let those comments slide off my shoulders and keep moving forward anyway because people matter to Jesus.

I've had to find some creative ways to work out God's calling on my life, and even in those times, God has been incredibly faithful. In fact, I used to preach to my stuffed animals as an early teen. In college, I preached to the walls of my dorm room. In seminary and even up to this day, I'll preach to the books in my library if I have to ... but preaching, teaching, and leading aren't everything. I also serve in a variety of capacities. In serving, I've learned much about listening to and obeying God, and I've noticed that in those moments of serving, conversations happen, relationships happen, and lives are changed.

At the end of the day, this is what it's all about: loving Jesus, loving people, and building bridges so that anyone and everyone can have the opportunity to realize and understand how very much Jesus loves them.

So, whoever you are and whatever your story is, know that God is deeply at work in your life. He sees, He knows, and He is able to do what others may deem to be impossible.

Sincerely,

A Professor who believes there is a story behind every name and title

Dear Student,

You emailed me today and said 1) I'm the first female Bible professor you've ever had (and you appreciate my teaching style and methods), 2) you don't personally know of any other females who have pursued theological education beyond the master's level, 3) you want to know how to traverse the journey of earning a master's degree (and maybe a Ph.D.) in a theological area and 4) you've been rejected by people close to you who don't understand your calling.

My response to you is, "When can we get together and chat?"

Today is a good day!

Sincerely,

A Professor who lives for investing in students' goals and dreams

Dear Sisters in Christ,

You were made for more. When someone tells you that you can't lead because you're a woman, lead anyway. When they say you can't preach or teach, do it anyway. When they say you're not meant to break through glass ceilings, break them anyway. When you're told that you are "less than" because you were created by God to be a woman, let those words roll off because you, too, were created in the image of God.

When someone tells you to "go home" because you're a woman, then shake the dust off your feet and go do what God has called you to do anyway. When vile, hateful words are spoken to you or about you, extend the love of Jesus to those around you anyway. Do not settle for anything less than who God created you to be. Show up. Take that risk. Rise to the challenge. Be courageous. You were made for more.

Sincerely,

Rev. Dr. Alaine Thomson Buchanan

Dear Student (almost 22 year-old Alaine ...
a much younger "me"),

Good morning! I'm writing to you today because I want to encourage you. I know that jumping into full-time ministry is your dream, and you're doing it, but it's been hard. You jumped in with both feet just a few months ago and are quickly realizing that you love leading and serving people, but you're not as fond of spending hours and hours with television and sound equipment. What you don't realize quite yet is that this first ministry position as a television director at a local church is going to prepare you for a wild and crazy journey with Jesus as you follow His call and leading.

Some people will love you. Some will hate you. Some will be kind to your face and then rip you to shreds behind your back. Let them do it and choose to love them anyway. Let the people, events, and situations in your life create a backbone in you so that you can be as hard as a rock and as gentle as a dove.

Opportunities will come and go. Titles will come and go. Positions will come and go. Friendships will come and go. Treasure what God has given to you, and when it's time to let go, then let go. Experience all the emotions that come with success and failure, with gain and loss. Let those experiences shape you to conform more closely to the character of Christ. Seek healing, forgiveness, and restoration (if possible). Try to accept what "is" and never give up hope for today and tomorrow. Use those experiences and emotions to make the world a better place and to further the kingdom of God.

Know, understand, believe, and live the reality that all people...ALL people...are created in the image of God and should be treated with respect and dignity. Realize your prejudices and biases and deal with them. Listen and learn from those who are different than you and respect their perspectives, even when you disagree with them. Pride will take you to places you never expected. Humility will do the same...just in a very different direction. Be intentional about choosing strength with humility. Some will initially view this as arrogance and pride due to their own experiences. Some will make all kinds of assumptions about you because of who you are and what you do. Love them like Jesus would anyway.

Unbeknownst to you, there will be times where God calls you to break through glass ceilings. Embrace the journey. Focus on Jesus. Keep moving forward. Hold on to the people who choose to stay with you despite what is going on in and around you. Love other people regardless of how they choose to interact with you. Following Jesus will cost you everything, and it will change your life for the better. Let God use your life and experiences to encourage others on their own journey. It will all be worth it. I promise you.

Someday, you'll be married and have a child. These people are gifts God has given to you. Love them well. You and your husband will be called to different ministries, and you'll be each other's number one cheerleader.

Your child, a son, will bring so much joy to your life, and he will challenge you because God has called him to challenge the status quo and to break through glass ceilings too … just like his dad and mom.

Finally, never ever forget that God loves you because you're you. Love God, love people, and embrace the journey for what it is. Never give up. Make the hard decisions…and follow after Jesus no matter the cost.

Sincerely,

Rev. Dr. Alaine Thomson Buchanan

For When You Want to Express
What's on Your Mind

Dear Student,

You and I had a difficult discussion earlier this week. You wanted an extension on an assignment that is due today, and I told you, "No." You expressed that I am heartless, that I don't understand what it's like to have a family, to be in school and to do ministry all at once, and that if I did, I would be willing to extend you some grace.

I told you that being in school is a large chunk of your ministry today and provides a glimpse into what future ministry could look like. Your investment now is going to increase your ability to minister in a variety of contexts later. I also told you that I believe in you and know that you can do this.

Today, you sent me an email to thank me and to apologize. You wrote that as soon as you turned your assignment in, the Holy Spirit reminded you that you had previously set aside some time today to spend with God ... and that the Holy Spirit told you that God helped you finish your assignment on time so that you could do just that. You thanked me for encouraging you to push through and to finish on time.

So, I have a couple of things to say to you: 1) Please don't assume that professors haven't "been there" before and that we don't understand. The reality is that we have been in similar situations, and we've also seen and watched God do what we thought was impossible. God is still on the throne, and we are still alive. 2) I pray your time with Jesus today is sweet and that it is filled with joy, peace, hope, favor, grace, and rest!

You did it! I am so very proud of you!

Sincerely,

A Professor who really has "been there" before

Dear Student,

You stayed after class today to ask me about my trip last week, so I told you and the others who were listening a little bit about what happened. You and other students who have had me in previous classes were (and are) aware about some of the healing process God has been taking me through over the past couple years. I told you one brief story about a conversation I had while at this conference, and the words you said in response were profound.

You said, "You know, Dr. Buchanan, it's okay to take a break from academia, if you need to. I'm sure whatever your book proposal was is really good, but to be honest, you really need to write about your own story. People's lives are at stake. Academia will always be here waiting for you. People may not be."

My dear student, I want to thank you for having the guts to speak the truth to me in love. You are one of the multiple voices that have expressed the same thing in different ways to me over the past two weeks. I have much to pray about and consider. The truth is that every single person really does matter to Jesus, and that message needs to be heard.

Sincerely,

A Professor who believes it is okay to be "real"
with students

Dear Student,

Several weeks ago, we faced an unfortunate situation with one of your assignments. I told you what the consequences were, and I also wrote, "I believe in you" because I do.

You responded with the words, "You are the second person in my life to tell me that (you believe in me)."

When I saw those words, I was initially speechless ... and then I began to pray for you that you would sense how much God loves you and believes in you and how much the people around you believe in you too.

I continued to push and challenge you and everyone else in our class all the way up to the very end, and you turned things around ... and you succeeded. I could not be prouder! Well done! Well done! Well done!

Sincerely,

A Professor who believes one word of encouragement can turn everything around

Dear Student,

Sometimes I wish students knew how much their words make a difference in the lives of their professors.

I don't think any of my students are aware that I am having one of those "I really don't want to teach today" days (those days are incredibly rare because I truly love to give and invest in other people), but today is "that" day.

... and then, during one of our regularly scheduled breaks, you said, "You know, Dr. Buchanan, this is the only class I'm in this semester where the professor gives us breaks but no one wants to leave."

That comment was enough to help me push through the rest of the class. I am so grateful!

Sincerely,

A Professor who appreciates students who love to learn

Dear Student,

My husband and I were talking about implicit bias a couple days ago (because everyone has implicit bias, whether they are aware of it or not). He asked me if someone had ever pointed out implicit bias to me, so I told him about a conversation you and I had several months ago.

I remember that you stayed after class one day, and I could tell by the look on your face that something was not right. I asked you if something was wrong and what I could do to help, and then you said, "I don't know if you realize that you do this, but every time I speak in class, your shoulders tighten up. You do that with one other student too. Anytime anyone else talks, your shoulders are relaxed. When your shoulders tense up, it makes me feel like you don't want me to talk or that you don't like me. Is that true?"

I remember the look of shock on my face, because I had no idea I was doing that. I apologized to you (I apologized to the other student too), thanked you for pointing this out to me, and told you how valuable you are to me and to our class. I promised to work on this because I don't ever want someone to feel like they are "less than." I also told you that you could give me a signal in class if you noticed my shoulders tightening up again (which you never did). I wish you could have seen the smile on your face at the end of our conversation. The trust that was built that day was incredible, and it was all because you had the courage to talk with me about this.

I am still so grateful for you and for that conversation, and I pray that others will have the courage to point out the implicit biases I have so that the light of Jesus can truly shine through everything I say and do.

Sincerely,

A grateful Professor

Dear Student,

"Thank you" are two of the most powerful words you could ever say/write to your professors. Sometimes, those two words mean the world to us. It lets us know that our prayers, late (and sometimes sleepless) nights, our constructive criticisms (aka grading), our responses to your emails, and our teaching (including the prep work) have mattered to you in some way. We professors believe in you, we wouldn't do what we do without you, and we are grateful for you too!

Sincerely,

A grateful (and very tired) Professor who has heard the words "thank you" a couple times today

Dear Student,

This is our third class (in a row) together. In our first class, we had to deal with plagiarism and really low grades, yet you insisted that you wanted to learn and to keep trying. In our second class, your desire to succeed pushed you through a challenging class, and you passed it. We are now in our third class together, and I recently finished grading your paper, and you earned a B on it!!! Wow!!!

I cannot tell you how proud I am of you! You kept focused, you kept working hard, and YOU DID IT!!! YES! YES! YES!!!!

Well done!

Sincerely,

A Professor who is so proud of you!

Dear Student,

In our class today, you presented your research paper and your reflections from visiting a worship facility for a religion outside of Christianity, which including interacting with an adherent of that particular faith community.

In the midst of your presentation, you said, "I realized that I was interacting with a real person who firmly believes in their religion, and I felt the love Jesus has for this person. I realized that this person needed to see Jesus in my actions and in my willingness to listen, so I asked questions. I listened, and then this person asked me about my faith. I got to talk a bit about Jesus, and it was all because I stepped out of my comfort zone, I chose to care about the person, I asked questions, and I listened first."

I am so very proud of you!

Sincerely,

A Professor who thinks religion is about people, people whom Jesus loves and who we should love too

Dear Student,

Last week, you contacted me to let me know that although you are unaware of the details surrounding my professional life, you sensed that you needed to pray for me, and you did. Then you told me what God showed you about my circumstances, and what God showed you was spot on. You called on some other former students to pray, and they are praying too.

Whether you realize it or not, God has raised you up to be a leader of leaders, to raise the arms of those around you, to intercede for those who are in challenging circumstances, and to extend the love of Jesus to everyone around you.

Thank you for reaching out to me. Thank you for praying for me. Thank you for your leadership and thank you for being sensitive to and listening to the leading of the Holy Spirit.

I firmly believe that whatever happens in this season will result in many people coming to know Jesus, loving God well and loving their neighbors the way Jesus does. God is good and faithful.

Sincerely,

A Professor who is humbled and grateful

Dear Student,

Today, you sent me an email to say, "Thank you" for investing in you last semester and to keep using my gift of teaching. Although you have no idea about what is going on in my life (professionally), you blessed me beyond measure today. Your note came at just the right time.

Thank you for saying "Thank you!"

Sincerely,

A grateful Professor

For the End of Class

Dear Students,

Sometimes, I have a class where I wish the "gathering together" part didn't end so quickly. Yes, all of us are thrilled when assignments have been turned in and the grading is done, yet there was something really special about your class. All of you are involved in some form of leadership. All of you participate in a variety of platforms. All of you were forced way out of your comfort zones in this class, and all of you embraced the journey I asked you to go on. Your ability and desire to learn from each other and invest in each other was humbling and amazing to watch.

I am so blessed to have been a part of your lives for a short time!

Sincerely,

A Professor who is humbled to have the opportunity to serve you

Dear Student,

When you take the time to say, "Thank you!" to your professor at the end of a class, it means the world to us. We believe in you. We're cheering for you. We are proud of you too!

Sincerely,

A very tired professor who is going to sleep well tonight

Dear Student,

You have a voice, and yes, you should use it. When it comes time to fill out the evaluation for your class, please be honest and tell the truth. If you have something positive to say, this is the time to write it down.

If you have something negative to say, please include a suggestion or two on how the professor or class can improve in the future. This is constructive criticism, and it is greatly appreciated.

Just remember that whatever score a professor receives and whatever comments are included go on the professor's permanent record, which cannot be changed or adjusted at a later time. These evaluations are oftentimes used by the leadership of the school in helping to determine whether or not the professor will have the opportunity to teach future classes at your school and potentially at other schools as well.

We are so grateful for you and your input. Thank you for using your voice!

Sincerely,

A Professor who appreciates the value of each student